Saint Frances Xavier Cabrini

Saint Frances Xavier Cabrini
Cecchina's Dream

Written by
Victoria Dority, MSC
and
Mary Lou Andes, MSC

Illustrated by
Barbara Kiwak

Pauline
BOOKS & MEDIA
Boston

Library of Congress Cataloging-in-Publication Data

Dority, Victoria.
Saint Frances Xavier Cabrini : Cecchina's dream / written by Victoria Dority and Mary Lou Andes ; illustrated by Barbara Kiwak.
    p. cm. — (Encounter the saints series ; 20)
  ISBN 0-8198-7092-7 (pbk.)
1. Cabrini, Frances Xavier, Saint, 1850–1917. I. Andes, Mary Lou. II. Kiwak, Barbara. III. Title. IV. Series.
  BX4700.C13D67 2005
  271'.9302—dc22

                                        2005002884

Published by Pauline Books & Media, 50 Saint Pauls Avenue, Boston, MA 02130-3491.

Printed in the U.S.A.

www.pauline.org

Pauline Books & Media is the publishing house of the Daughters of St. Paul, an international congregation of women religious serving the Church with the communications media.

2 3 4 5 6 7 8 9   11 10 09 08 07 06

Encounter the Saints Series

Blesseds Jacinta and Francisco Marto
Shepherds of Fatima

Blessed Pier Giorgio Frassati
Journey to the Summit

Blessed Teresa of Calcutta
Missionary of Charity

Journeys with Mary
Apparitions of Our Lady

Saint Anthony of Padua
Fire and Light

Saint Bernadette Soubirous
Light in the Grotto

Saint Edith Stein
Blessed by the Cross

Saint Elizabeth Ann Seton
Daughter of America

Saint Frances Xavier Cabrini
Cecchina's Dream

Saint Francis of Assisi
Gentle Revolutionary

Saint Ignatius of Loyola
For the Greater Glory of God

Saint Isaac Jogues
With Burning Heart

Saint Joan of Arc
God's Soldier

Saint Juan Diego
And Our Lady of Guadalupe

Saint Katharine Drexel
The Total Gift

Saint Martin de Porres
Humble Healer

Saint Maximilian Kolbe
Mary's Knight

Saint Pio of Pietrelcina
Rich in Love

Saint Thérèse of Lisieux
The Way of Love

For other children's titles on the Saints,
visit our Web site: www.pauline.org
Encounter the Saints Series

CONTENTS

"Cecchina" for Short

It was July 15, 1850. Agostino Cabrini was already out threshing wheat as the sun rose above his farm in northern Italy. He paused to pray. "Heavenly Father, I offer you my day. I also have a favor to ask. Stella is showing signs that our baby is coming...but it's two months early. Please allow this child to remain with us, since four of our children are already with you. Please...permit this child to live and grow up to serve you." When the sturdy peasant turned back to his work, a flock of snow-white doves encircled the grain. In his attempt to scatter the birds, Signor Cabrini caught one in his strap.

The farmer gently untangled the dove. He could feel its tiny heart thumping wildly. "Come and see this little one before it returns home," he called to his children, who were playing nearby.

"Oh, Papa, how beautiful!" cried Rosa. "Look, Maddalena! Papa brought us a visitor. Where's Giovanni? Come and touch the dove. Feel how soft it is! Giuseppe! Francesco! Come see what Papa has!"

The children crowded around their father. "Can we keep it for a pet?" they pleaded.

"No, no," Signor Cabrini smiled. "The Lord made the birds of the air to be free. We must allow our little friend to return to its family now." As he opened his hands to release the dove, an urgent cry echoed across the fields.

"Agostino! Agostino! The baby is coming! Hurry!"

Signor Cabrini broke into a run. "Watch the children, Rosa!" he shouted over his shoulder. Later, as more doves encircled the farmhouse, Signora Cabrini gave birth to a tiny daughter as small and fragile as a dove. The townspeople of Sant'Angelo Lodigiano always believed that God had sent the flock of gentle white birds as a sign that the child born that day was special.

Since their new daughter was so tiny and in danger of death, Signor and Signora Cabrini wanted her to be baptized as soon as possible. That evening she was taken to the parish church and given the name Maria Francesca. Because it was such a long name for a tiny baby, everyone called her "Cecchina" for short.

Fifteen-year-old Rosa realized that neither her mother nor her new baby sister were very strong. This made her very protective of Cecchina and more helpful to her mother. Although Maddalena was the oldest child in the family, she had been born with brain damage. And so it was Rosa who soon became known as Cecchina's second mother. Under her care Cecchina slowly grew stronger and gained weight.

"Rosa, you're a great help to me," her mother confided one day. "But you mustn't forget your own dreams. Your father and I know that you want to become a teacher. Father Dedé has told us about the Daughters of the Sacred Heart in Arluno. These sisters train young girls to teach. We think it's time for you to begin your studies with them."

After four years of study at the sisters' boarding school, Rosa happily returned home with her teacher's diploma. She eventually opened a school for the children of Sant'Angelo right in the Cabrini farmhouse. It was there that Cecchina was educated and developed her own love for teaching. Although she was sick a great deal, she was still able to follow her lessons from her room. Rosa made sure that Cecchina never missed anything.

By the time Cecchina was five, she was attending daily Mass with her mother and Rosa. She watched her big sister and copied everything she did. When Rosa returned from receiving Communion, she covered her face with her hands. So did Cecchina. But she made sure to spread her fingers apart so that she could still see what was happening. If Rosa made the Sign of the Cross, Cecchina did too. She even scratched her nose whenever her big sister did!

One day, Cecchina decided to follow her mother and sister up to Communion. Rosa caught her in time and made her go back and sit in the bench. "Just what did you think you were doing, Maria Francesca?" Rosa asked after Mass. (Rosa called Cecchina her full name when she wanted to be extra serious.) The little girl looked up in innocent surprise. "I was going to receive Jesus with you and Mama," she matter-of-factly answered.

Another time, Cecchina watched Rosa go into the confessional. She decided to do the same. But once inside, she had her doubts. "Father!" she exclaimed. "Where are you? I can't see you."

"I'm here behind the screen," the priest answered kindly. "What do you want to tell me?"

"Father, why can't I receive Jesus in Communion like Mama and Rosa? I love him too, and Rosa taught me all my prayers. I want to do what Jesus tells me to do and not always what Rosa makes me do!"

"My child," Father Dedé answered, trying to hide the amusement in his voice, "Jesus gives us people to help us to learn and to understand what to do. Jesus wants you to listen to Rosa and do what she says. Isn't she a good sister to you?"

"Yes, Father," replied Cecchina. "She teaches me a lot about Jesus. I want to be a teacher just like Rosa. I want to teach others about Jesus and how much he loves us."

"Well, then, you must listen to Rosa," replied the priest. "Think of it as Jesus talking to you. Go now, and may God bless you."

"May God bless you, too, Father!" Cecchina cheerfully answered.

On her way out of the confessional, the child peeked under the other curtain and saw Father Dedé. She waved as he smiled at her, and he waved back. Cecchina would always remember that day.

Rosa was very strict with her younger sister. She especially impressed upon her the importance of using every opportunity to pray and offer little sacrifices to Jesus.

"Ouch! Ouch!" six-year-old Cecchina would complain as her sister combed her naturally curly hair into long braids. "Why are you pulling my hair so tight? And why do you have to put so much oil on it?"

"Because your hair doesn't want to obey!" Rosa would answer. "It keeps sneaking out of the braids. You don't want the other girls to feel badly because they weren't blessed with curly hair, do you? Besides, all those curls might make you as proud as the peacock who likes to show off. If it hurts you too much to sit still, offer it up to Jesus for some poor sinner."

Cecchina was always relieved when Rosa finally ended her "sermon."

Many years later, when Mother Frances Cabrini was well into her fifties, she used to laugh and say, "I don't think I'll ever have gray hair.... Rosa pulled it so tight, it never had a chance to do anything, let alone turn gray!"

2

THE SEED IS PLANTED

Every evening, the Cabrini family would gather around Papa. While Rosa and Mama mended or folded clothes, knitted or crocheted, Papa would read from *The Annals of the Propagation of the Faith,* a magazine that featured stories of missionaries who worked in far off lands, spreading the Good News of Jesus.

Young Francesca heard about people and places and things that she didn't even know existed. She learned how people in the Orient ate with chopsticks. She found out why Japanese women dressed in brightly colored kimonos, while women in China usually wore loose, drab trousers as they worked in the fields. The child was fascinated when she saw how the Chinese and Japanese wrote the letters of their alphabet. She learned that there were explorers who had gone into the jungles of Africa and discovered many different tribes living there. Francesca became curious about the customs and cultures of people who lived so far away. It was as if she had discovered a whole new world. At night, she would dream of these far-away places. She especially dreamed of going to China as a missionary. She wanted with all her heart to teach the people there about how much God loved them and wanted them to be a part of his plan of salvation. *Some day I'll go to China,* she told herself, *some day.*

"Cecchina, why are you so serious?" her father asked one evening.

"Papa, everyone should know how much Jesus loves them," Francesca answered, her blue eyes shining with excitement. "I want to tell them, Papa! I want to go to the missions and tell them! Please, Papa, let me go. I already know how to read and write. I even know some French..."

"Slow down, my little one," Signor Cabrini replied with a smile. "You're still too young to travel to such far-away places. For now, you can pray and offer up your work and sacrifices for the missionaries."

Not long after, Father Dedé announced that a missionary named Father Gino would be coming to speak at the parish church. Francesca was full of questions as she and Rosa walked home from Mass. "Rosa, I thought that a missionary is someone who goes to other countries where people have never heard about God, or about how he sent Jesus to save everyone. Father Dedé said that Father Gino's mission is in the mountains near Italy. Don't the people there already know about God and Jesus and Mary? Why didn't Father Gino go to another country? Don't missionaries have to cross oceans?"

"So many questions!" laughed Rosa.

Before Rosa had a chance to explain, Francesca began answering her own questions with a wisdom that impressed her older sister.

"Wait...I think I understand, Rosa! A missionary can bring God's Word *anywhere* that it needs to be brought. Missionaries can travel far away, to people who've never heard about God. Or they can be like Father Gino and help those who already know God to understand better how much he loves us and wants us to love each other. I think missionaries bring the Word of God to different people in different ways."

"You're right Cecchina," replied Rosa with a smile. "Some missionaries teach. Some help sick people. Some missionaries help build houses. But they all bring people the Word of God in their own way."

Francesca's large eyes sparkled with joy as she and her sister continued their talk. "I liked the story about Saint Francis Xavier that Papa read to us the other night. He went really far away, and the people he helped had never even heard about God. Maybe he didn't get to Japan, but God let him see it from where he was when he died. And best of all, he became a great saint. When I grow up, I want to be a missionary, too!" announced the resolute, almost nine-year-old Francesca.

"You shouldn't be worrying about becoming a missionary, Cecchina," Rosa advised. "Just concentrate on being a good follower of Jesus for now! When the time comes for you to choose what to do with your life, God will let you know."

As Rosa was talking, Francesca was carrying on a conversation with Jesus in her heart. She decided that from that moment on she would begin preparing herself to become a missionary. *My life will be different now, Jesus,* she prayed. *When I'm in school, I'll work harder and try to learn as much as I can. I'll be kind and help the other children who need my help. I'll also be good and obedient at home, helping Mama and Papa and my brothers and sisters. I'll pray for the missionaries every day.*

Rosa realized from the expression on Francesca's face that her sister was deep in thought and hadn't heard a word she had said. How could she tell her that there were not yet any female missionary congregations whose sisters traveled to lands across the ocean? *When the time comes,* Rosa thought, *the Lord himself will need to make it clear to Cecchina that her missionary adventures will have to be confined to prayer.*

Francesca stood absolutely still and quiet for almost two minutes. Finally, she looked up at Rosa. "All right," she said. "For now, I'm going to pray every day for the missionaries. They have a very big job to do for God, and they need his help in a special way."

Francesca continued to think about her favorite missionary, Saint Francis Xavier. She even began to compare herself with him. Of course, Francis Xavier was much older, much healthier, much more educated, and, although she had never found his physical description in any book, she imagined that he was not quite as skinny as she! But Francesca was still sure that someday, somehow, Jesus would show her how she could also be his missionary.

Later that week, the Cabrini family went to listen to Father Gino speak of his work. Francesca was so excited about all she heard that she couldn't sit still. After the talk, Father Dedé introduced her family to the visiting priest. Francesca could hardly control her enthusiasm. She was finally meeting a real missionary!

"Father Gino!" she enthusiastically announced, "I'm going to be a missionary someday too! I'm going to bring the good news of God's love to others!"

Rosa laughed. "Why, Francesca Cabrini! I've told you before that you're much too sickly, much too ignorant of life, and much, much too young to even be thinking of it. You're still only in elementary school..."

Father Dedé was surprised at Rosa's reaction. As he placed his hand on Francesca's head, she whispered softly, "Father, I want to be a missionary!" He smiled at the innocence of the young child and saw the future in her eyes. "Well then, Cecchina," he replied, "become what God is whispering to your heart."

What began as God's gentle whisper, Francesca later described as his persistent call. God had planted a small seed that was destined to grow into something big and beautiful.

3

VIOLETS FOR SAIL

Francesca would often visit her uncle, Father Luigi, who was a parish priest in a nearby town. His church and rectory were located near a river whose current was very swift. It was the perfect place for a little girl with big missionary dreams to play.

One day, when she was nine, Francesca was down on the riverbank playing her "missionary game." She would make paper boats and fill them with wild violets, pretending that the flowers were her "missionary sisters" and that she was their mother superior. It was a game she never tired of. On this particular day, Francesca was sending her "sisters" to China, to bring the Gospel and the love of God to those who had never experienced them.

"Good-bye, Sisters!" she cried as the current carried the little vessels away. "Bring Jesus and Mary to everyone you meet!"

Standing on the river's edge and waving energetically to her departing missionaries, Francesca suddenly slipped on the muddy

"Bring Jesus and Mary to everyone you meet."

bank. She lost her balance and tumbled into the icy, rushing water.

"Cecchina! Cecchina! Wake up! Cecchina!"

Francesca opened her eyes to see her uncle frantically bending over her. Why was he so excited? And why was she so terribly wet and cold? Francesca began to shiver. What had happened? She remembered waving to her missionary-violets...and then plunging into the water. Her thoughts were interrupted by Father Luigi's voice.

"Thank God you're all right! You gave us all quite a scare, young lady. It's a good thing that Signor Rossi saw you fall into the river. He sent his son to call me while he tried to rescue you. Now here's the strangest part...Signor Rossi ran down the bank, following the current so that he could reach out to you as the water flowed by, but he found you lying on the bank. What I want to know is...who pulled you out? How did you get up on the riverbank?"

Wide-eyed Francesca looked calmly at her uncle and replied, "It was my guardian angel, Uncle Luigi. I remember falling into the water and crashing against the rocks. Then, all of a sudden, I felt my angel pick me up and put me on the riverbank. When I opened my eyes, he was gone."

"That could be, Cecchina," her uncle said with a shake of his head, "but guardian angels usually like to use other people to help them. Did anyone help your angel? Can you remember?"

Francesca furrowed her brows. "Absolutely not!" she insisted. "My angel pulled me from the water all by himself!" Since they never found who had helped her, Francesca always believed that it was her guardian angel who had saved her life.

"Well, we're not going to give your angel any more extra work," Father Luigi concluded. "From now on you must not play down by the water. It's much too dangerous."

That was just fine with Francesca, who developed a lifelong fear of water from that day on. But her troubles weren't yet over. Upon returning home, Francesca came down with a very high fever. The doctor was even doubtful that she would live. He prepared the Cabrini family for the worst. Partly because she was already in poor health, and partly because infant and child-hood deaths were very common in the nineteenth century, Agostino and Stella also readied their children for the loss of Francesca.

Stella had given birth to eleven children and, by that time, seven of them had already died—some in infancy, others as toddlers, or as young teens. Death was an experience they had all shared, so the Cabrini children were well prepared to send another sister to heaven to pray for them.

For nearly a week, Francesca suffered very high temperatures and delirium. Agostino and Stella prayed that God would spare the life of their Cecchina. Father Dedé spent many of those sleepless nights with the Cabrini family. He knew how much they would miss this little one. And he knew how much he would miss her, too. Everyone was overjoyed when Cecchina's fever finally broke and she was out of danger. As a result of the accident, however, Francesca's already poor health suffered another setback. Bronchitis would plague her for the rest of her life.

4

MAMA AND PAPA SAY "YES"

"Rosa," called Father Dedé one morning after Mass. "Please ask your parents if I may visit tomorrow evening. I have something to discuss with the four of you. Cecchina, I think you'll be very interested in what I have to say." Father Dedé smiled and gave the thirteen-year-old a quick wink before turning to walk up the brick path to the rectory.

The next evening found the pastor at the family's farm. After the children noisily welcomed him, Signor Cabrini offered Father Dedé a chair. Signora Cabrini brought him a cup of steaming black coffee.

"Agostino, I'd like to talk with you about Cecchina's education," the priest began. "I know the fears that you and Stella have concerning her poor health. But even though she missed so many days of school, she still scored high in her state exams. She's always been a good tutor for the little ones, helping Rosa with the children who were having difficulties."

The pastor paused and took a long swallow of Stella's strong coffee. "I think that the

Lord has blessed Cecchina with a fine mind, a generous spirit, and a heart that's over-flowing with love," he continued. "We're entering a new age, Agostino. You and I probably won't be around for the next century, but hopefully the children will! The young must be prepared to be strong and faithful Catholics. Let's try to help them to do just that—through education. I feel that the Lord has something big in mind for our little Cecchina. I have no idea what it is, but she must be prepared."

Father Dedé was beginning to wonder what Signor and Signora Cabrini were thinking. But he didn't give them a chance to respond. "Rosa attended the teacher-training school with the Daughters of the Sacred Heart in Arluno," he hurried on. "If I'm not mistaken, Sister Victoria, who taught religious education at our parish, is now in Arluno. Cecchina, you remember Sister Victoria, don't you?"

"Yes, Father," Francesca beamed, "very well."

"Anyway," the pastor continued, "the school is close enough to allow Cecchina to come home for the holidays. She'll receive a marvelous education from the sisters—both for her mind and for her soul. I'm sure that she'll blossom in ways that only God knows. We've just got to give her the chance." Father Dedé leaned forward and looked expectantly at the four faces in front of him. Francesca waited in suspense. Rosa, along with Signora Cabrini, seemed lost in thought. Perhaps he had said too much....

Stella was the first to break the silence. "You're right, Father," she sighed. "We've always encouraged our children to make the best use of whatever gifts of talent and grace God has given them. I worry about Cecchina's health, about her safety, about so many things.... I guess worrying comes natural to a mother. I know that someday I'll have to let each of my children go, but it's very difficult when the time comes.... I believe that Cecchina is ready to go to Arluno. But that's just my opinion. Agostino? Rosa? What do you think?"

Agostino studied his wife. He knew how much of a sacrifice she was making in agreeing to allow their youngest daughter to leave home. He, too, had gone through the anguish of watching seven of their children die. Thirteen-year-old Giuseppe and eighteen-year-old Francesco had been the last to go to heaven. Agostino, too, worried about their sickly Francesca.

"I think Arluno is a splendid idea!" he agreed. "Cecchina must move beyond the town limits of Sant'Angelo and primary school. She needs to spread her wings."

Is Agostino thinking about those doves that circled the farm at Francesca's birth? Father Dedé wondered. The priest turned to Rosa. "And how do you feel about it, Rosa?"

"I'm just as happy over Francesca's having the opportunity to go on with her education as I was to study in Arluno, Father. The change will be good for her in every way."

Father Dedé sat back in satisfaction. "Well, now that you'll be going away to school, Cecchina, I'd better start calling you 'Signorina Cabrini.' It sounds more grown-up, don't you think?"

"Oh, Father! You can call me by any name you like!" Francesca exclaimed in her joy.

Thank you, Lord, for this chance! Francesca prayed that night. *Now you must help me to do my best for you. I want to learn as much as I can and become the person you want me to be. And when problems come, I'll give them all to you, Jesus. You're much better at solving them than I am.*

As she thought about going away to school, Francesca realized that up until this point in her life she had had many teachers. From her mother and father and Rosa, she had learned about the very loving God who watches over us and made the world for us to use and enjoy. She had learned about God's wonderful plan of salvation for all people and the role that the Church plays in this plan. She had also learned how to love God by loving her neighbor. Signor and Signora Cabrini had always taught their children that since God had been so good to them, they must be good to others. Francesca often accompanied Rosa or her mother to deliver a basket of food to a family struggling to make ends meet. At other times they would go to an elderly person's house to clean or do the laundry.

From her father, especially, Francesca had learned to love the land. Signor Cabrini had taught her the necessity of the right kind of soil for growing good crops. He had taught her about different types of flowers and plants. "This is chamomile, Cecchina," he would say. "It can be picked and used for tea or to soothe the nerves. The aloe plant is also important. Its gel is very helpful in treating dry skin and even burns."

Once, when a bee had stung her younger brother, Giovanni, Francesca had watched as Papa applied mud to lessen the pain and swelling. Everything Francesca had learned from her father, especially about the medicinal properties of various herbs, was very valuable knowledge. It would be of great assistance to her in her life as a missionary.

Father Dedé, Francesca's spiritual guide, had taught her to depend on Jesus for answers to important questions concerning major events in her life. When she would ask the priest for his opinion about something, Father Dedé would usually reply, "Well, Cecchina, why don't you ask Jesus what he thinks? You must learn to depend more on him than on people to help you understand and decide things." Francesca learned this lesson well. It was one that she never forgot.

Her priest-uncle impressed upon Francesca the importance of fair wages, safe working conditions, and decent work hours for laborers. Father Luigi also explained many teachings of the Church regarding the just treatment of people. He and Francesca often discussed what "fair wages" meant, or how "safe working conditions" and "decent hours" affected the workers. As Francesca grew older, she understood much more and appreciated Father Luigi's dedication to his working-class parishioners. She also understood why his parishioners loved their parish priest so well.

While her family and Father Dedé taught Francesca how God loved her and how she should love God, it was at the sisters' school at Arluno that she learned an even greater love—that of the Sacred Heart of Jesus. Francesca's love for Jesus would direct her life until the very end.

5

PATIENCE AND HONEY

"Rosa, what's it like at boarding school?" fourteen-year-old Francesca asked as the two sisters did the dishes. "Are there many girls there? Do you think they'll like me? I mean, it's a little scary to go to a new school where I don't know anyone...." Francesca dropped her towel and stared blankly out the window. Without waiting for an answer, she went on. "What if I get sick and miss class? How will the sisters be able to take care of me? Even worse, what if they send me home!"

Rosa dried her hands on her apron. "Don't think such thoughts," she chided, giving Francesca a hug. Holding her close, she took a handkerchief and dabbed at the tears now streaming down the younger girl's cheeks. Rosa well remembered her own first-day fears at the boarding school.

Once Francesca had regained her composure, Rosa switched back to her older sister/teacher mode. "Now, what kind of trust do you have in God?" she asked. "If the Lord has allowed you to come this far, Maria Francesca Cabrini, do you doubt that his power will see you through to the end? Boarding school won't be so frightening. For one thing, living in the dormitory will be like living in a large family...."

Although Francesca had her fears about not being able to come home every evening, she remained firm in her decision to attend school in Arluno. Besides learning the newest methods and techniques in teaching there, Francesca also learned the secret of order and discipline in the classroom. At that time, Bishop Francis de Sales was being raised to sainthood in the Catholic Church. He had been outstanding for his kindness and gentleness, and the sisters tried to impress upon their future teachers that these were the tools to use in keeping order in the classroom. Francesca observed her teachers using only kind and gentle words, even with girls who stretched their patience.

One day, after trying so hard to explain a scientific concept to one of the girls, Francesca confessed to Sister Victoria, "I'm having a hard time being patient with Carla, Sister. I've explained the same problem at least five times! I think I'll lose the rest of my patience if I have to explain it again...."

"How many times do we read in the Gospel about how slow the Apostles were to understand something?" the teacher replied. "Did Jesus become impatient? And do you remember what one of Saint Francis de Sales' favorite mottos was?"

"Yes, Sister," answered Francesca. "He said that he could catch more flies with a spoonful of honey than with a barrel of vinegar. I remember you explained that if someone uses sweetness and gentleness, instead of harshness or cruelty, the point can be made just as well. The lesson may take longer to get across, but it will last longer, too." Francesca smiled knowingly. "I guess it's much better for me to spend my energy helping Carla to understand that it's the green leaves that make food for plants than it is to be thinking that she's just not as quick as the rest of the class."

Sister Victoria nodded. "Remember this, Francesca, it's only through love and patience that we give our students any feeling of success. Not every child is gifted by God with the same talents or intelligence. But every child is gifted by God with the same right to learn as much as his or her capacity will allow. As teachers, we must look to Jesus as our example and try to discover the treasure within each person."

"I'll remember that, Sister. And I'll try," promised Francesca.

We know very little about the years Francesca spent in Arluno. But we do know that she loved school and that she studied hard. We also know that she tried to join in as many activities as she could. Historical records show that she was the president of the Sodality of the Blessed Virgin Mary. Yet, by her own admission, she was very shy during her schooldays. Once, when referring to her years in boarding school, she admitted, "I was so shy, I hardly dared to raise my eyes."

As always, Francesca's health was poor. School records testify that she was absent a great deal. She suffered from the usual bouts of fever and bronchitis, but she always managed to keep up with the rest of her class.

In 1868, at the age of eighteen, Francesca returned home to Sant'Angelo with her teacher's diploma and her state license. She was now a qualified teacher. She knew that Rosa could use her help in teaching the children of Sant'Angelo. But there was something else on her mind.

"Rosa," Francesca confided one day as they were taking a walk, "when I was in

Arluno, it seemed so clear to me that the Lord was calling me to the convent. I love the sisters' devotion to the Sacred Heart of Jesus and the wonderful work that they do for children. Yet, when I spoke to Mother Superior, she told me that my poor health was a sign that God was *not* calling me to become a Daughter of the Sacred Heart! I was so sure that this was what God wanted me to do. Do you think I was wrong?"

"Of course, good health is important for a religious sister," Rosa answered thoughtfully. "Without it, how could you carry out your mission? But did you ever consider that the Lord might have another project in mind for you? I once thought that I was being called to the convent, too. But God had other plans. My special work is to teach the children here in Sant'Angelo and help Father Dedé with religious instruction classes. You can always consecrate yourself to the Sacred Heart without becoming a sister, Francesca. It won't be a public consecration, but Jesus will know. And that's what's important. Just keep praying. I'm sure the Lord will show you what he wants when the time comes."

Francesca put her complete trust in the Lord. *I don't know or understand, dearest Jesus,* she prayed, *but you do. I must learn to be as patient with you as you are with me. I'll wait and pray...especially for patience.*

It would be twelve long years before Francesca would receive Jesus' answer concerning her life's mission. Until then, he would use everything that was happening to her to teach her many important lessons.

6

THE DREADED POX

"Stella, I really don't feel well," Signor Cabrini admitted one morning. Signora Cabrini noticed that her husband's face was ashen. "Sit down, Agostino," she encouraged. "I'll get you a cup of black coffee. You'll feel much better after you drink it..."

When Stella returned, Agostino was on the floor. "Rosa! Francesca!" she frantically called. "It's your Papa!..." The girls came running. Stella wept as she cradled Agostino's motionless body. Francesca tried to console her, while Rosa ran for help. When the doctor arrived, he had some upsetting news. "I'm afraid that your husband has suffered a severe stroke, Signora Cabrini. There's not much that we can do." Signor Cabrini passed away that same year, 1870. And his wife followed soon after him. Now Rosa and Francesca were left to care for their oldest sister Maddalena. Their only living brother, Giovanni Battista, became a college professor and eventually moved to Argentina.

With the death of her parents behind her, Francesca continued to live her quiet, regulated life helping Rosa with the little school on the family's farm. Then, in 1872, a notice arrived from the government. Though she would have wished it otherwise, Francesca's life was about to drastically change.

The Italian government in the region of Sant'Angelo Lodigiano had also undergone a major upheaval. The Austrian government had controlled a part of northern Italy, but certain Italian groups wanted to get rid of the Austrians, and they staged a rebellion. As a result, Italy again unified its regions under one government.

The new political authorities decreed that teachers who had received their licenses under the former Austrian government now had to renew them. This meant that all educators had to take certain courses and pass difficult exams in order to obtain the renewal. Until the licenses were renewed, no instructor was allowed to teach.

Every day for four months, Francesca and Rosa traveled to the town of Lodi to attend the required classes. Having completed this course of study, the two Cabrini sisters took the examinations, passed them, and received the necessary certification to continue teaching.

"Rosa, I'm so happy that everything worked out," Francesca confided. "Now we'll have some peace and quiet for a change." Little did she suspect that the Lord had something very different in mind.

That spring, as the two sisters were returning home from morning Mass, one of their young students ran up to them. She seemed to be in a panic. "Oh, please, Signorina Rosa and Signorina Francesca!" the little girl pleaded. "Mama is very sick and so are my brothers... Papa said to ask you to come and help us..."

Francesca hugged the child and said very gently, "Calm down, Angela. Getting yourself all upset won't help your mother or your brothers, will it?"

"No, Signorina. But will you come... please?"

"Of course we will," Francesca answered.

"Now Angela, run and call Dr. Di Franco," Rosa broke in. "We'll meet you at your house."

Francesca and Rosa exchanged worried glances. They had heard that there was an outbreak of smallpox in the Lodigiano region. "I hope I'm wrong," Rosa murmured, "but it sounds like the dreaded pox!"

The doctor confirmed Rosa's worst suspicions: the smallpox epidemic had reached their town. After visiting Angela's family, the Cabrini sisters were the first to take care of the sick. Since the outbreak had forced them to close their school, the two teachers became visiting nurses. Rosa and Francesca brought food and medicine to those who were stricken with the virus. They also did whatever needed to be done in the homes of the sick. They bathed the sores of the victims, tidied up, and, since smallpox is very contagious, they washed, boiled, or burned soiled linens, clothing, and bandages. They helped families who had lost loved ones to arrange funerals, and then they mourned with them.

Besides bringing food and medicine to the sick, they brought the love of God to all they met. Many fears were calmed and many deaths were peaceful because of the serenity of these two fearless women who put into action Jesus' desire that his followers visit the sick and bury the dead.

But none of this was easy. Francesca found that cleansing the sores of the sick actually repelled her. She felt very badly

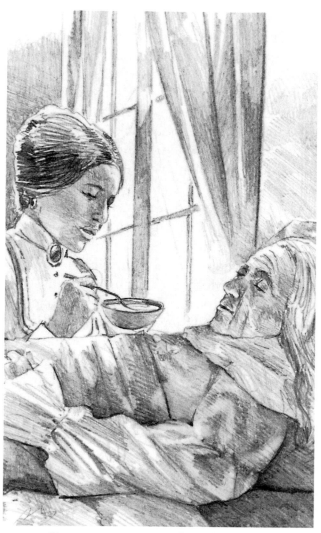

Francesca courageously cared for the smallpox victims.

about this, because she was sure that she wasn't hiding her repugnance very well. All through her life Francesca would try never to let her personal feelings interfere with any act of charity that she felt was prompted by God. She herself eventually contracted smallpox, but Rosa took such excellent care of her that when Francesca recovered, her skin was not marked by even a single scar.

Later on, when Francesca began her missionary work in America, she decided to have nothing to do with hospitals. One night, she had a "dream" in which she saw the Blessed Mother cleaning wounds and emptying bedpans. Francesca approached Mary and asked her why she was doing such work. The Blessed Virgin looked her in the eye and simply answered, "Because you refuse to do it." Francesca understood. Later, in 1891, she opened her first hospital in New York, to serve the medical needs of the Italian immigrants. Today, Cabrini Medical Center strives to meet the needs of all who come seeking help, from the homeless in need of medical care, food, or clothing, to those suffering from the AIDS virus, or terminally ill patients who require hospice care as they prepare to meet God. In later years, Francesca's religious sisters would also open nursing homes to provide care for the sick and elderly who could no longer live at home.

7

JUST TWO WEEKS...

The letter that was to change Francesca's life arrived one Sunday morning in 1872.

"Who was it?" Rosa asked when her younger sister returned from the front door holding an official-looking white envelope.

"Father Antonio Serrati from Vidardo has sent me a letter by messenger," responded Francesca in a puzzled tone. "The man who delivered it says he'll be returning to Vidardo on Thursday, if I'd like to send a reply. That's strange...I don't even know this priest...."

Rosa was just as surprised. "Now you've gotten me curious," she laughed. "Well, hurry up! Open it!"

Francesca tore open the envelope and began to read the letter aloud. When she was nearing the end, she interjected, "Listen to this part, Rosa! 'Since our public school teacher has become ill, there is a vacancy to be filled. I have taken the liberty, on behalf of our town, of inviting you to come for an interview to fill this position. I await your reply by return messenger. Sincerely yours, Father Serrati.'"

"How in the world did he get my name?" Francesca exclaimed. "And how could I possibly help him? I have enough work to do right here in Sant'Angelo. The children lost so much class time during the smallpox epidemic. Now we need to work doubly hard to get them caught up in time for the state examinations!" Francesca slipped the letter back into its envelope and dropped it on the table. "I'll answer it later," she sighed.

By the next day she had penned a respectful "thanks, but no thanks" note to Father Serrati. She sent it on its way with the messenger that Thursday. Three days later, Father Dedé asked her to stop by the rectory.

When Francesca arrived, the pastor led her to the parlor. "There's someone whom I'd like you to meet, Francesca. He's an old friend who is in need of assistance, and I think you're the one who can help him."

As they entered the room, a priest rose from his chair to greet them. He was of slight build and did not immediately impress Francesca.

"Father Serrati," began her pastor, "may I present Signorina Francesca Cabrini, one of Sant'Angelo's finest teachers, and an outstanding member of our parish.

Francesca, this is Father Serrati, the pastor of the parish in Vidardo. It seems that their public school needs a teacher, and when he asked me if I knew of anyone, I gave him your name."

Francesca felt her heart pounding. *If only the floor would open and swallow me up!* she thought. Smiling weakly, she shook the visitor's hand, wondering if he had already received her reply.

"So, Signorina Cabrini, we meet at last!" Father Serrati said cheerfully. He was struck by Francesca's penetrating blue eyes and gentle smile. "I'm afraid I'll never know of Francesca's ability to teach, Father Dedé," he said turning to his friend. "She has already refused my offer by letter. I came here with the hope that together you and I might be able to convince her to change her mind. She would only need to serve as a substitute teacher until the town council finds a permanent replacement. It would be a matter of two weeks at the most."

As he spoke, Francesca completely changed her impression of the small man. What he lacked in stature, he made up for by his forceful speech and dignified manner.

Father Dedé, being very gracious, invited Father Serrati and Francesca to discuss the matter over some coffee. As the pastor offered her a cup, she noted a twinkle in his eyes. She knew what he would prefer her to do.

Francesca looked from Father Serrati to Father Dedé. "I thank you both for your great confidence in my teaching ability," she said slowly, "but I'm afraid that I must refuse your request. Sant'Angelo is recovering from the smallpox epidemic, and my sister and I still have a great deal of schoolwork to make up."

"Francesca," began Father Dedé, "Father is only asking you to go to Vidardo for two or three weeks. Surely Rosa can do without you for that long." He paused and decided to try another approach. "You've always admired missionaries. Couldn't you consider this time in Vidardo as a kind of missionary journey?" Silently the priest begged the Lord to touch Francesca's heart. He didn't have long to wait.

Francesca was also praying. Looking at the two priests before her, she took a deep breath. "All right," she agreed with a smile, "I'll go for two weeks. As Rosa once told me when I was a child, 'a missionary brings the Word of God to those in need,' and certainly Vidardo's children are in need."

8

THE SISTERS OF PROVIDENCE

Francesca succeeded so well with her innovative teaching methods and her patience that her "two weeks" in Vidardo stretched into two years.

In the meantime, Father, now Monsignor Serrati, had been transferred to a larger town. There was an orphanage in this town that was in serious trouble. Because it was in his parish, Monsignor Serrati was responsible for the financial problems that it incurred. He knew that the orphanage needed new administration. And he knew just the person who could help set things right. But first he would need to speak to the bishop.

Arriving at the residence, Monsignor Serrati was escorted to the office where Bishop Domenico Gelmini was busy working. Once the introductory greetings were over, Monsignor Serrati came right to the point. "When I needed a teacher for the public school in Vidardo, Your Excellency, Father Dedé recommended a young woman from Sant'Angelo. After much persuasion, she finally came and stayed on. Her unique blend of patience, love, and modern teaching methods, combined with a very strong faith and spirit of prayer, worked miracles. She managed to touch even the most stubborn—parents and children alike. She even converted the mayor! Her help in the parish was just as invaluable."

Monsignor Serrati stopped and studied the bishop's face for signs that his words might be having an impact. Detecting none, he continued, "As you know, there's an orphanage in my parish. It was begun some time ago by a woman named Antonia Tondini. She has since donated the house and property to the parish, but with the understanding that she is to live there until she dies. It's a very complicated situation! The house needs repair and renovation. The orphans need food and clothing. The local people are very good to the children, Your Excellency, but they don't like that Tondini woman." Monsignor Serrati shook his head. "It seems that she's acquired many debts without ever bothering to pay them. I'm convinced that the orphanage, called the House of Providence, needs new administration. With your encouragement, Bishop Gelmini, perhaps Francesca Cabrini would be willing to help."

The bishop thought for a moment. "I'm very familiar with the House of Providence and with Antonia Tondini," he replied. "I've been trying for a long time to decide what to do about that place. I've often wanted to close it, but then I think of the orphans. At least those poor little girls now have shelter, food, and clothing, as insufficient as these may be. But perhaps you're right, Monsignor. Perhaps the House of Providence needs new blood. This Cabrini woman you mentioned sounds almost too good to be true. However, I'm willing to let her try to work things out. Would she consider coming here? I'll leave it to you. Do whatever you can to bring your Francesca Cabrini to Codogno."

Monsignor Serrati asked Francesca. And she refused. Again, Monsignor Serrati enlisted the help of Father Dedé.

About a week or so later, Rosa and Francesca were leaving the parish church after Mass, when Father Dedé called after them. "Francesca, would you be so kind as to meet with me in the rectory after lunch? I have a favor to ask of you."

That afternoon, Father Dedé explained Monsignor Serrati's dilemma to Francesca and asked if she would go to Codogno to help the orphans. It wasn't easy for Francesca to leave Rosa and Maddalena, whom Rosa would care for until Maddalena's death. But she found that she couldn't refuse her pastor's request, especially when he again compared the situation to a missionary adventure.

Francesca had often said that hard work was good and even improved her poor health. And there was certainly no lack of work at the orphanage. Before Francesca's arrival, Monsignor Serrati had managed to get a few dedicated young women of the parish to help. Like Francesca, they desired to become religious sisters and were already trying to live the religious life. The group became known as the Sisters of Providence. Under Francesca's leadership they accomplished so much that even Bishop Gelmini was surprised.

When Francesca discovered that so many of Codogno's people, especially the women, were illiterate, she wanted to help. She called her little group of collaborators together. "We've been asked by Monsignor Serrati to teach some of his parishioners to read and write," she explained. "I'm most concerned about many of our young women. As you know, we've begun to teach our orphan girls sewing—everything from basic stitching to fancy needlework. Our goals are simple. We want to enable the girls to clothe their own families once they're wives and mothers, or to master a skill as a means of financial support. Since we've already established the classes, why don't we allow the young women of the parish to join us?"

Francesca and the Sisters of Providence began many activities in the parish. Besides teaching religious education classes, they prepared the younger children for reception of the sacraments and provided activities for the older children. They also held classes for young women who had not had the opportunity to complete their education. Francesca and her companions were zealous for the kingdom of God!

During the period that Francesca lived and worked in Codogno, her thoughts were always on far-away mission lands. She often spoke of missionary work to some of the other young women. A few of them even began to share her dream. The Lord was quietly working to prepare Francesca for the missionary journey of a lifetime.

9

MOTHER FRANCES XAVIER

Because of their desire to serve the Lord in a special way, Francesca and her companions eventually asked both Bishop Gelmini and Monsignor Serrati to allow them to make vows as true religious sisters. The bishop and the monsignor agreed, on the condition that Francesca would serve as the superior of the new community.

"Your Excellency," Francesca said, "I would like, with your permission, to add the name Xavier to my baptismal name, in honor of Saint Francis Xavier."

The bishop smilingly replied, "Yes, my daughter. From now on you shall be known as Mother Frances Xavier Cabrini."

Over the years, Bishop Gelmini had come to admire this little blue-eyed woman. He had seen her strong faith and her deep spirit of prayer. He was sure that living and working with Antonia Tondini had been a cross for Francesca. He had heard rumors about the verbal abuse that Antonia heaped on Francesca. The bishop often questioned Francesca about Antonia's behavior, but her response was always the same: "All is as the Lord wills it to be." The conversation would then turn to another subject. Never in all the years that Bishop Gelmini had known Francesca Cabrini did he ever hear her speak unkindly about someone.

The people who lived and worked in the neighborhood of the orphanage, however, had much more to say about Antonia Tondini. Merchants and delivery people were often the recipients of her sarcastic remarks or rude and even vicious behavior. Neighbors testified that Antonia frequently slapped the orphans. All these incidents were reported to the bishop.

Although Francesca didn't approve of Antonia's behavior, she knew that confronting her would only make things worse. Francesca would often speak to her young women about setting a good example to everyone they came in contact with. She knew that there were some people whom only God could change, and prayer would be their means of conversion. Antonia Tondini was constantly in her prayers.

One day Bishop Gelmini called Francesca to his residence. After inquiring about her health and various other matters, the bishop was silent for a minute or two.

Finally he spoke. "Mother, I'll come right to the point. I've tried for seven long years to remedy the many problems associated with the House of Providence. When Antonia Tondini was running the orphanage, she allowed debts to grow and the house to fall apart. I've done everything in my power to keep it going..."

"Your Excellency has been a great help to us, and we are all very grateful," Francesca interjected. "To be fair to Sister Antonia..."

The bishop held up his hand. "Wait until I've finished, please. You've accomplished impossible feats with that place, Mother. You've managed to win back all the merchants that Tondini alienated. Not only that, but you've paid them all. You've also managed to get major repairs done on a building that was in critical disrepair and is still in need of further renovation."

Francesca sat with her hands clasped on her lap, feeling very uncomfortable with the bishop's praise. "Your Excellency," she said quietly, "if anything was accomplished, it was accomplished by the Lord working through me. I'm only his instrument."

The bishop smiled at Francesca's humility and shook his head. "I've made my decision, Mother. The House of Providence will close at the end of the year. We can talk about placing the remaining orphans with some of the good families of Codogno who would be willing to take them."

Bishop Gelmini remembered that Francesca had once told him of her great desire for missionary work. He also knew how much she had animated the small group of Sisters of Providence. He did not wish to lose them or their work with the poor. "Mother Cabrini," Bishop Gelmini continued, "I'm well aware of your dream to become a missionary. I'm also aware of your desire to continue living the religious life. Up to now, only men have been called "missionaries." Yet, didn't God send his angels to the women with the news of the resurrection of Jesus? I don't know of any congregation of missionary sisters, Mother. So it seems to me that you must begin one!"

All Francesca could think of in that moment was Father Dedé's challenge to her so many years before, *If you want to be...then become!*

Francesca smiled broadly at the bishop. Her heart pounding with excitement, she replied, "I shall look for a house immediately, Your Excellency."

10

THE CEMENT FACTORY

Now that the bishop had given her permission, Francesca began in earnest to look for an appropriate house. Before she undertook any important responsibility, she always brought it to prayer. So she went to the nearby Franciscan church and sought the help of heaven.

Kneeling before the image of Our Lady of Grace, she prayed, "Dearest Mother Mary, please help me! I must find a suitable house in which to begin our new religious family. I'm relying on your help."

There was in Codogno a very old Franciscan friary that had been abandoned since the seventeenth century. Francesca decided to visit it. Other than the one or two small rooms being used as shops on the first floor, the huge complex was empty. The structure appeared sturdy enough, but of course Francesca didn't know very much about buildings. She looked around as much as she dared without attracting attention to herself, then returned home.

On her way back to the House of Providence, where she and the small group of sisters were packing and cleaning up in preparation for their move, she again stopped by the church. Once again, she knelt in front of the image of Our Lady of Grace. "Thank you, dearest Mother," she prayed. "You've helped me find the perfect place. Now please help me convince Bishop Gelmini to obtain it. Sacred Heart of my beloved Jesus, I place all my trust in you."

When Francesca reached the House of Providence, Monsignor Serrati was waiting for her. He seemed extremely happy about something and was very eager to speak with her.

"Monsignor, how nice of you to stop by!" Francesca greeted him as the two sat down in the parlor. "Antonia was kind enough to allow us to stay here until we can find a house in which to begin our new missionary institute dedicated to the Sacred Heart of Jesus." Francesca's eyes flashed as she spoke. "But I must see Bishop Gelmini as soon as possible. I think I've found a place."

"That's just what I'm here to talk about, Mother," Monsignor Serrati replied. "I've already made a down payment on a convent. You and the other sisters can move in immediately! I wanted to surprise you. Not only that, I also want to give you this offering of 10,000 lire. You'll need at least that much money to begin with."

Francesca stared at the excited priest in stunned silence. She knew that she would have to gently tell him that he was not the one to decide on a "suitable house" for the sisters. As the foundress of a new religious family, she had to make the decisions. She had new responsibilities, and she must assume them. At the same time, Francesca, who was usually very docile, didn't want to appear ungrateful or arrogant. She fervently prayed for the guidance of the Holy Spirit.

Finally, the little nun stood. "Thank you, Monsignor," she said in a resolute voice. "It was very kind of you to be so concerned for us. I know that you only want to help, but I've already decided on the place. I just need to discuss it with the bishop."

Monsignor Serrati knew from Francesca's tone of voice that she was determined. He also new of her deep faith and trust that the Lord was directing her actions. The priest thought it best not to question her. "I had no idea, Mother!" he replied. "Well, take the 10,000 lire anyway. I'm sure you can put it to good use. And if I can be of any further assistance, please don't hesitate to ask."

Relieved that the priest respected her judgment, Francesca smiled. "Thank you for all you've already done for us, Monsignor. You've been a true friend in the Lord. Of course, I won't hesitate to ask for your help."

Monsignor Serrati pressed the money into Francesca's hand. "Well, I must be on my way," he said. "Don't forget now, if you need anything, you know where to find me. God bless you."

Francesca couldn't wait to tell the bishop about the building she had discovered. She lost no time in walking the short distance to his residence, praying to the Blessed Mother as she went.

When she arrived, the housekeeper promptly led her into the front parlor. As soon as the bishop entered the room, Francesca rose and began speaking very quickly. "Wait until I tell you where the Blessed Mother led me, Your Excellency! She brought me to the building that will be the motherhouse of our new congregation. It's ideal, as I'm sure you'll agree when you see it. It's an old Franciscan friary that was abandoned when Napoleon was in power. It requires some minor repairs, but it will suit our needs perfectly."

After listening patiently, Bishop Gelmini responded, "I have great faith in your judgment, Mother, but I'd feel better if you'd allow me to see about obtaining the house. I'd like someone to evaluate the strength and structure of the building. If it dates back to Napoleon's time, it really should be examined by an expert."

Bishop Gelmini hired Carlos Martino, a young architect from Milan, to inspect the property and make an offer to the owner. "Be very careful and don't tell him why you're interested in buying the friary," the bishop cautioned. "He'll raise the price if he finds out that the building will be used as a convent. And whatever you do, don't let him know that I'm involved. Then he'll surely charge much more than the building is worth!"

The architect arrived at the address that Bishop Gelmini had given him. His first stop was at the little repair shop on the ground floor. "I'm looking for the proprietor," he told a gray-haired man who was working on the axle of a wagon. "I've heard this building is for sale, and I'm interested in it."

The older man straightened up. "I'm the owner, Bruno Fiore. I *might* want to sell if the price is right. What do you want to do with the place?"

"Well, Signor Fiore, I'm looking for a very large building that I can use as a storage space," answered Signor Martino. "This is perfect. If you would care to negotiate, you'll see that I'm willing to give you a fair price."

Now's my chance to get rid of this monstrosity of a building! Signor Fiore thought. *I've got to be careful, though, and not appear too anxious.*

"This building is very old, Signor Martino," Fiore boasted. "It goes back to the time of Napoleon..." As soon as the words were out of his mouth, the owner realized that he had taken the wrong approach.

"Signor Fiore, I have every confidence that if there's any structural damage due to the building's advanced age, you will be willing to make a price adjustment," the architect calmly responded. "In the meantime, I'm prepared to offer you this," and, scribbling a figure on a piece of paper, Martino held it out.

Fiore's dark eyes widened. "I'll take it! I'll take it!" he nearly shouted. "The place is yours! Just give me a day or two to clear out my shop. By the way," Fiore added after he had calmed down a bit, "just what is it that you want to store here?"

"Materials to make concrete," Martino casually replied.

Bishop Gelmini was amused by the architect's report of what had happened. After hearing back from him, the bishop sent a messenger to the House of Providence to ask Francesca to come and see him. He related the story of the young architect's adventure with the building's owner. "But Signor Martino was correct, Your Excellency," Francesca laughed at the conclusion. "With our cement we're going to build God's kingdom all over the world!"

11

BEGINNINGS

On November 10, 1880, the little community that had gathered around Mother Frances Xavier Cabrini moved into its new home. These first Sisters—Salesia, Gesuina, Agostina, Colomba, Veronica, Franceschina, and Gaetanina—were members of the group of Sisters of Providence who had asked to profess the vows of religious life. They had shared Francesca's missionary dream at the orphanage, along with her desire to serve the Lord. As the years passed, many more young women would come to join them.

"Mother, it will be so nice to finally be in our very own place!" exclaimed Sister Salesia as they unloaded the wagon containing the few articles they had brought from the House of Providence.

"I'll help you take some of these beds upstairs, Mother. It's good to be home, isn't it?" Sister Agostina echoed.

Francesca looked at her eager young sisters. These were the souls that the Sacred Heart of Jesus had entrusted to her care.

These were the seeds that would blossom into a new missionary institute for the Church. "My daughters, we must thank the Sacred Heart of Jesus and his most holy Mother for allowing us to find this house," she told them. "We must remember that whatever happens, Jesus and Mary will always be with us. So, it isn't just *our* very own home, it's *theirs*, too! Now, before we start moving the furniture in, why don't you all take a quick tour of the house?"

When the wagon was finally emptied, and the few pieces of furniture put in place, the sisters sat down to their first meal in their new convent. By that time, the sun was beginning to set. As twilight darkened, Sister Colomba began looking for a lamp.

"Mother, you wouldn't believe what we did!" she finally burst out. "We didn't even bring a lamp with us. I've searched everywhere and have only come up with this half-burned candle..."

"Well, I guess we'll have to make do with that," smiled the foundress. And the sisters were happy in their poverty.

From their very first day in the old friary, the sisters placed themselves completely in Francesca's hands. She was to them, as everyone now called her, Mother Cabrini, and they had absolute confidence in her ability to lead them in the missionary adventure that was about to begin.

"Daughters, we need a nice statue of the Sacred Heart of Jesus for our chapel," Mother Cabrini commented during that first week in Codogno. "I have a beautiful painting, but I think that a statue would be more appropriate. Please pray that we can get one."

Later that afternoon, Monsignor Serrati stopped by, bringing with him a large and very beautiful statue of Our Lady of Grace. The sister who answered the door led him into the room that was being prepared for the chapel. Mother Cabrini was on a ladder, putting the finishing touches on the windows.

"Mother," Monsignor enthusiastically announced, "I've brought this lovely statue of the Madonna for your new chapel. Just tell me where to place it. Oh, I see a space...right over the altar!"

Mother Cabrini hurried down from the ladder. She certainly *didn't* want to refuse her friend's gift, but she *did* want to save that niche over the altar for an image of the Sacred Heart. What a predicament! When Monsignor tried to place his statue above the altar, however, he discovered that it was too tall. He was disappointed, but Mother Cabrini knew that it had been an answer to her prayer.

"Don't worry," she said. "I have just the right painting to put there. What better reminder for the Missionary Sisters of the Sacred Heart than a picture of the Sacred Heart of Jesus?" She handed Monsignor Serrati the painting, and he placed it in the niche in which he had intended to put the Madonna.

"As for Our Lady of Grace," Mother Cabrini continued, "why, we'll give her her own private area!" So saying, she asked the priest to place the beautiful statue on one of the side altars.

On November 14, 1880, just four days after their arrival, Monsignor Serrati celebrated the first Mass in the sisters' new convent. One month later, the bishop of Lodi officially approved the Missionary Sisters of the Sacred Heart of Jesus as a religious congregation. Though from her childhood Francesca had dreamed of an institute like this, she could hardly believe that her dream had finally come true!

To this day, the convent at Codogno, Italy, is still used by the Missionary Sisters. It's now a House of Spirituality, still offering others the spiritual "cement" that helps them grow in and share with others the knowledge and love of the Sacred Heart. On display there are the bed and chair that Mother Cabrini used, as well as some of her personal items. Visitors may also see the first Rule of the Missionary Sisters of the Sacred Heart of Jesus, written in Mother Cabrini's own handwriting.

12

THE WORLD IS TOO SMALL

Once the sisters were established in Codogno, they set right to work. They opened a school and were soon accepting both boarding and day students. In addition to the school, Mother Cabrini and her sisters cared for the orphans of the town.

There was much to be accomplished, and the members of the new religious community wanted to do all they could for God and his people. As she observed her sisters working with the townspeople, Mother Cabrini recognized the gifts and talents that each possessed. This knowledge would be especially useful later on, when she sent her sisters to foreign countries to open new missions.

Mother Cabrini's enthusiasm to accomplish great things for Jesus gave her new energy. That energy was contagious and spread to her sisters. After the Missionary Sisters of the Sacred Heart of Jesus had been in Codogno for two years, they were asked to begin a school in the neighboring town of Grumello. From there, they expanded to

Mother Cabrini saw God in the face of each child.

Milan and other cities and towns in Italy. They could never go very far from their motherhouse in Codogno, though, because they had not yet received the Church's permission to move beyond the boundaries of the Diocese of Lodi.

Mother Cabrini held on to her ideal of being a missionary, even though, for the time being, she had to confine her work to nearby places. She knew that she was just an instrument in the hands of the Lord. When the right time came, he would work things out.

One afternoon, as the children were playing in the schoolyard, Mother Cabrini was talking to Monsignor Serrati. Good as he was, Monsignor disagreed with Mother's missionary vision. He wanted to restrict her community to local works, if not just to Codogno, then just to the Diocese of Lodi.

"Monsignor, there are five more young women who wish to enter our community, but we've run out of space!" Mother Cabrini excitedly explained.

"I'm not in favor of you accepting any more applicants, Mother," the priest said shaking his head. "You have plenty of sisters to accomplish the works that you're now doing. Frankly, I don't think you need any more. If you keep growing, you'll end up with more sisters than you have works!"

Mother Cabrini was beginning to feel upset. She silently asked Jesus to keep her temper in check. "Monsignor, if the Lord is blessing the Missionary Sisters of his Sacred Heart with applicants, don't you think it's a sign that he wants them to serve him in this community?" she finally replied. "There will never be enough sisters to do all the work that Jesus wants us to accomplish!" She was absolutely certain of this and was determined to make her friend understand. "No, Monsignor, I believe that if we're being blessed with young women who want to join our family, it's the Lord's way of giving us his approval. With all due respect, we live in a world that has no boundaries in the eyes of God," she continued in a very serious tone. "As a young child I would sit at my father's feet listening to stories of missionaries who traveled all over the globe to bring the love of God to others. The world is too small for me, Monsignor, and I won't rest until the work of the Lord is completed in me. I'll go where he leads and do the work that he wants done."

The priest was at a loss for words. He felt very humbled in the nun's presence. As he prepared to leave, he gave Mother Cabrini his blessing. Then, taking her hands, he looked into her expressive eyes. "I've known you a long time, Francesca Cabrini, and I know that once you set your heart and mind on something you believe is God's will, you let nothing get in your way. I will try to keep an open mind if you'll do the same."

13

ROMAN ADVENTURE

It was 1887, and the Missionary Sisters of the Sacred Heart of Jesus had been in existence for seven years. Mother Frances Xavier Cabrini wanted to eventually extend her works to the Orient. But she realized that in order to be taken seriously, she needed the approval and support of Pope Leo XIII.

"Sisters," she explained one day, "we must obtain the approval of the Holy Father in order to be officially recognized as a missionary institute. We also need to open a house in Rome. Please pray for these graces when you go to chapel. I'm going to speak with Monsignor Serrati and Bishop Gelmini about the matter."

"Mother, you want *too* much *too* quickly!" Monsignor Serrati exclaimed when Mother Cabrini told him of her plans. "You must be satisfied with the works and houses that you already have. How can you even think of going to Rome!" The priest paced the floor as he continued. "You haven't much to offer to the Holy Father in the way of being a missionary congregation, you know. If you really want to impress the pope, you should wait until your institute is more mature. You need to develop resources that will assure your financial stability. After all, Mother, we live in a world that requires money to function."

"No, Monsignor," Mother Cabrini answered calmly. "We live in a world that requires God to function. I'm going to speak to Bishop Gelmini. Perhaps he'll understand why I must go to Rome."

Unfortunately, Bishop Gelmini's reaction was not much different than Monsignor Serrati's. He too wanted to limit the sisters' works to his Diocese of Lodi.

"Mother, it's not an easy task to begin a convent in Rome," he argued. "To do so you have to obtain the permission of the cardinal in charge of these matters. You also need sufficient funds and personnel to maintain such a house."

Mother Cabrini furrowed her brow in thought. She looked up at the bishop. "Your Excellency, if it's the Lord's will that we are approved, it will happen. If it's not, then it won't. Surely you wouldn't be afraid to let us try, would you?"

Bishop Gelmini reflected a moment. *What if I'm standing in the way of God's will?*

he mused. "Mother," he finally said, "if the Lord wishes your religious congregation to be approved by the pope, then there is absolutely nothing that will stop it from happening. No, I'm not afraid to let you try to obtain approval. Go to Rome...with my blessing!"

Although neither Monsignor Serrati nor Bishop Gelmini shared Mother Cabrini's global missionary vision, both eventually approved her decisions. Both men certainly recognized that the Lord was working in and through the foundress.

Once in Rome, Mother Cabrini and Sister Gesuina, her traveling companion, went to a convent of the Franciscan Sisters. Their Mother Foundress, Sister Mary of the Passion, was a friend of Mother Cabrini's. Mother tried to stay with the Franciscans whenever she could.

Cardinal Lucido Parocchi was the person whom the pope had delegated to decide which congregations of sisters would be allowed to open a new convent or school in the city of Rome. Mother Cabrini soon made an appointment to see him.

"Mother," Cardinal Parocchi began, "before you give me the reasons why you should open a school here, I must tell you that I'm absolutely against such an action. There are much older, more experienced, and, I will add, much wiser congregations that have never opened even one house or one work in Rome. What makes you think that you can succeed where others haven't?"

The little nun wasn't about to give up. "Your Eminence," she countered, "don't you agree that children must be educated? Isn't the education of all Catholics, especially Catholic women, who will someday be the mothers of families, important?"

"Yes, of course. But your timing is all wrong. There are far too many religious houses and Catholic schools in Rome already. The best thing you can do is return to Codogno and serve the Church there."

Jesus, please help me! Mother Cabrini prayed in her heart. *If it's your desire that we begin a house in Rome, do something to change the cardinal's mind. I place this intention in your Sacred Heart.*

If the determined foundress had had 500 thousand lire at her disposal, starting a house in Rome wouldn't have been a problem. But without the money, it seemed that nothing could be done. Over and over again Mother Cabrini was advised to return to

Codogno and continue her work there. In the meantime, she had submitted for approval the Rule which she had written for her religious congregation. Mother asked Cardinal Parocchi if she might remain in Rome until she received an answer about the Rule. She also asked him if she could use this time in Rome to open a school. "You may stay here in Rome until you receive word about your Rule," the cardinal replied. "But as for opening a school, I'll have to refer the matter to the pope when he returns to the Vatican." Within a few weeks, however, Mother Cabrini was allowed not only to open a house in Rome, but was offered the administration of a school as well!

A little over four months later, Mother also received the Church's approval of her religious institute. Now, she was finally able to begin the work that the Sacred Heart of Jesus had placed in her heart.

14

To the West!

Positive news of Mother Cabrini and her Missionary Sisters of the Sacred Heart continued to spread throughout Italy. Bishop Geremia Bonomelli, who was doing wonderful work on behalf of Italian emigrants, greatly admired Mother Cabrini. Through him, she met Bishop Giovanni Battista Scalabrini. Bishop Scalabrini had dedicated himself to assisting Italians who had immigrated to the Americas. He hoped that Mother Cabrini would be able to collaborate in this work. The two bishops and the foundress were soon to become the leading advocates of persons who had left their Italian homeland in order to better their economic status.

During this time, Bishop Scalabrini was writing much about the dreadful conditions his people had to endure in America. His words were so powerful that they moved the heart of Pope Leo XIII. When the Holy Father received a request from Mother Cabrini to speak with him, he welcomed her warmly.

"Your Holiness, my dream has always been to leave my native land to bring Jesus to people who have never heard of him," Mother explained. "It is my heart's desire to accompany six of my sisters to the Orient. With your permission, we will prepare to leave soon."

"My dear daughter," Pope Leo responded, "my heart is heavy with worry about our Italian brothers and sisters living in America. They are like sheep without a shepherd; there is no one who can understand them. They are being treated worse than common criminals. I've heard that many are forced to live in subhuman conditions, with up to ten people sharing one room. They cannot find means to support themselves or their families." The pope leaned forward as if to emphasize the seriousness of what he was about to say. "English is difficult for them, and they are not well accepted by the Catholic parishes because of the language barrier and cultural differences. This is especially painful since the Church means everything to them. Therefore, Cabrini, think not of going to the East, but to the West!"

Mother Cabrini left the audience with much to reflect on and pray over. She had wanted for so long to go to China, but now many of her own people were in such need. *Perhaps Jesus really does want us in America,* she concluded.

Mother was eager to speak with her sisters that evening. "I believe that our desire to become true Missionaries of the Sacred Heart of Jesus and to travel to other lands is about to become a reality!" she excitedly announced. "The Holy Father is asking us to go to America to work among our own people and bring the love of Jesus to them. Let's prepare ourselves to leave as soon as possible."

Since the work of the sisters was well known and respected, many influential persons had become friends and benefactors of the institute. When Mother Cabrini and her sisters were ready to travel to America, the Lord sent the right people to their door. One day, a gentleman appeared at the convent. "Mother, I've heard of your plans to sail to America to give aid and comfort to our countrymen. I'm the owner of a shipping line and would like to offer you a stateroom for your travels." Mother Cabrini was very grateful for the offer and readily accepted. Because of her childhood accident in the river, she had a great fear of deep water.

Knowing that she and her sisters would have good accommodations on board ship helped her to feel more secure.

Soon, all of the preparations were completed. The Missionaries of the Sacred Heart of Jesus were ready to leave their homeland. The sisters set sail from Milan for New York on March 20, 1889.

"My dear daughters, let's stay on deck for a while," Mother Cabrini advised when the rolling of the ship began to make the sisters feel queasy. "The cool ocean air will help."

"Mother, are you sure Archbishop Corrigan wants us in New York?" asked Sister Concetta as they gazed out over the vast sea.

"Yes," the foundress confidently replied. "I have his letter right here. The Holy Father and Bishop Scalabrini assured me that Archbishop Corrigan will have everything ready for us when we arrive. It will be so good to bring our people comfort! The Sacred Heart of Jesus is leading us to our new mission. Come, let's pray the rosary to our Lady for calmer waters."

During their voyage Mother Cabrini and her sisters ministered to the other passengers. Mother spent most of her time in steerage, the section of the ship reserved for passengers who paid the lowest fare. Here she cared for the poor Italian immigrants, helping those who were sick, calming the fears of those who were afraid, and praying with all who wanted to pray. Mother Cabrini never went down to steerage without bringing something to give to her people, especially to the children.

One night, there was a knock at her cabin door. "La Madre! La Madre! You must help us!" Opening the door, the little nun found three very frightened sailors. "Please, Madre, ask your Sisters to pray! The storm is very bad, and we're in great danger! We don't want the passengers to know or there will be panic on board."

"We'll do all we can," Mother Cabrini reassured them. "I'll pray for your strength and courage. Put your life in God's hands. Trust him."

Mother quickly called the other sisters. Huddled together in the stateroom, they were afraid that the boat was actually going to capsize. Everyone was very seasick and could hardly walk.

"My daughters, we must be strong!" Mother Cabrini encouraged. "It's a frightening situation, but it's important that we help to keep the other passengers calm. In order

"The Statue of Liberty!"

to do that, we must commend ourselves to the Sacred Heart and Our Lady, Star of the Sea. Jesus calmed the waters for the Apostles, and he will calm them for us if we ask him with a courageous heart."

The terrible storm lasted for two and a half days. Many passengers became very ill. Some were even injured. The sisters, although frightened themselves, bravely did their best to give aid and comfort to others. They also helped the people to pray. Their fellow passengers admired their courage.

When the storm was finally over, the sky cleared and the waters calmed. The passengers asked the sisters to pray the Rosary with them in thanksgiving for their safety.

Mother Cabrini and her exhausted daughters arrived in New York harbor on a foggy, winter day. The date was March 31, 1889. At the sight of the Statue of Liberty, the little group forgot their fatigue and fears. As the sun was setting, the sisters joined their hearts and voices and sang the *Ave Maris Stella*. From that time on it became their custom to sing this hymn to Our Lady, Star of the Sea, every night.

15

NEW YORK

Once their feet were firmly planted on American soil, Mother Cabrini and her sisters were met by two Scalabrini Fathers. These priests belonged to the religious congregation which had been founded by Bishop Scalabrini. "Buon giorno, Sisters. Welcome!" exclaimed Father Dante. Gathering up their luggage, the sisters followed the priests to Saint Joachim Rectory. There they were served a traditional Italian meal.

Mother Cabrini and her sisters enjoyed the warm hospitality of their countrymen. They shared stories of their travel adventures, and of the many nights they were rocked vigorously to sleep by the ocean.

"Well, Father, it's getting late, and we're quite tired," Mother finally said. "We would appreciate it if you would show us to our convent."

A moment of nervous silence followed. Then Father Dante blurted out, "But, Mother, there seems to be some mistake...there *is* no convent prepared for you and your sisters! Didn't you receive the message?"

"Father, whatever are you talking about?" the foundress asked, making an effort to keep her voice calm. "We've traveled a very long way at the request of the Holy Father. Bishop Scalabrini assured me that everything would be in order when we arrived. Now, please, Father, kindly tell us where we are to spend the night."

"Well," replied a very red-faced Father Dante, "for tonight, at least, you'll have to use public lodging. I'll contact Archbishop Corrigan about the situation in the morning."

"Thank you, Father, but I can assure you that I'll be contacting the good archbishop myself," Mother Cabrini responded.

After getting over their initial shock of not having a convent to go to, the sisters were taken to a boarding house. There they experienced firsthand what the Holy Father meant by the "deplorable conditions" in which immigrants in America lived. Instead of having a peaceful and restful night's sleep, they came face to face with rats, roaches, and bed bugs! The living conditions were worse than those they had experienced aboard ship. "Sisters, pull up your skirts so that they don't drag on the floor. It might help to keep our visitors off our clothes," Mother Cabrini practically advised. "Above all, don't let the lamp burn out. Bugs and rodents like these are afraid of light."

Some of the sisters took turns trying to rest while the others prayed. It was almost impossible to sleep. The sisters never grew accustomed to their "visitors," but they quickly learned how to deal with them. Even more disturbing were the night noises of the boarding house. These helped the sisters understand what was happening to the people, their people. As sounds of screaming, bottles breaking and children crying pierced the darkness, the little community prayed for guidance and strength.

At first light, Mother Cabrini and Sister Concetta arrived at Archbishop Corrigan's residence. While Mother was presenting her documents from Rome, the archbishop appeared somewhat exasperated. "Excuse me, Mother," he said rather impatiently, "I don't want to seem disinterested, but I did send you and Bishop Scalabrini a cable stating that there was no reason for you to come all this way. We have enough religious sisters already working here in New York. Perhaps, if you hurry, you can catch the next steamer back to Italy."

"Thank you very much for your concern, Your Excellency," Mother Cabrini responded in a calm, deliberate tone. "But since the Holy Father has sent me here, I will only return if His Holiness calls me back to Italy. This is where I was sent, and this is where I will work!"

When Archbishop Corrigan saw the look of determination on the little nun's face, he knew that he had met his match. Mother Cabrini would not be deterred from her mission to serve the immigrants and fulfill the desires of the Sacred Heart of Jesus. The sisters soon had a convent of their own.

On a warm May night, as the community was in chapel thanking Jesus for having changed the mind and heart of the archbishop, there was a knock at the door. A few moments later, Sister Serafina tapped Mother Cabrini on the shoulder and pointed to two shabbily dressed little girls who were being led in. Mother's heart was touched at the sight of these children. Josephine, the oldest, explained that their mother had died and that their father couldn't take care of them. He had to work long hours digging tunnels. There were many nights when he couldn't come home. The girls were often left alone and forced to beg for food. "Don't worry, my little ones," Mother Cabrini comforted them. "You now have a home, and each sister will be your mother. I'll find your father and make all the arrangements with him."

It was at this moment that Mother knew, without a shadow of a doubt, that her mission had begun. She lost no time bathing and feeding the little girls. Since they had no change of clothes with them, she even used her own petticoat to make a dress for each of them. As Mother Cabrini watched them fall asleep that night, she carried on a conversation with Jesus in her heart. *Thank you, my Lord, not only for your blessings, but for the challenges you allow us. They help to make us stronger day by day.* The two girls thrived because of the love and care of the sisters. Josephine grew up to become a Missionary Sister of the Sacred Heart of Jesus, spending her entire life in the loving service of others.

16

GOD'S WELL RUNS DEEP

"Those Missionary Sisters never turn away any child who needs help." The good news spread quickly throughout Little Italy, the section of New York where most of the Italian immigrants lived. More and more children were brought to the sisters with the hope that they would have a better future. It was difficult for many parents to admit that they could no longer care for their children. In some cases, mothers or fathers had died because of the diseases that plagued the crowded city neighborhoods. Most of the immigrants were forced to work in environments where no importance was given to their safety or health. This led to a great number of deaths among the immigrant community.

Mother Cabrini and her sisters did what they could for the immigrants. They went into the factories, mines, and tunnels bringing food, water, and words of comfort to the workers. In the evenings, before their night prayers at the convent, the sisters discussed the adventures of the day. They also talked

*Mother and her sisters helped the immigrants
in every way possible.*

about the problems they had encountered and the ways they could improve their service to the poor immigrants. During those conversations, Mother Cabrini would often think of her uncle, Father Luigi, and the many talks they had had about these same problems in Italy.

The Missionary Sisters of the Sacred Heart of Jesus continued to teach hundreds of children each day, as well as to provide for the orphans. Since their school building was still not ready, classes were held in the church. The children used the benches as desks. In spite of all the hardships, they received a well-rounded education not only for their minds, but for their hearts and souls as well. The sisters also taught them the life skills that would be so helpful to them in the future.

Mother Cabrini went on to establish many schools, hospitals, and orphanages in other parts of the United Stated and abroad. Like the school in Little Italy, these quickly became gathering places for Italian families. Besides teaching children, the sisters would help families do whatever needed to be done. They took care of their spiritual needs as well, assisting them in rediscovering their faith. For many Italians, daily poverty made life unbearable. Struggling to provide for their families left little time for anything else. The sisters would often go into the homes and pray with the people, bringing God to them. The immigrants trusted the Missionary Sisters before anyone else, and often shared their pain and struggles with them.

It was Mother Cabrini's dream to have her orphans live in the country, where fresh air and space would help them grow and develop in a peaceful and secure environment. But this dream would take some time to come true.

One day, Archbishop Corrigan took Mother Cabrini and a companion on a trip along the Hudson River. He brought them to visit another community of sisters whom he wanted them to meet. As they stood on a hill overlooking the river, the archbishop pointed to the land on the opposite side. "One day, Mother," he said, "you shall have that land on which to build your orphanage."

Mother smiled and quietly nodded. She was thanking Jesus for having shown her this beautiful sight. The property that Archbishop Corrigan was pointing out belonged to the Jesuit Fathers. The place was called Manresa and was the home of the Jesuit House of Studies. Unknown to Mother Cabrini at that time, the property would soon be up for sale.

Throughout the next few months, the estate along the Hudson River was always on her mind. She believed in her heart that Jesus wanted her to have that land for the children. Her dream of fresh air, sunshine, and space became more persistent each day. Finally, she approached the priests who owned the property.

"Mother, I have to be very honest with you," the priest in charge admitted. "The reason we're selling this property at such a low price is that we haven't been able to find a water source. It's very difficult to carry water from the river each day. If you still want to buy the land in spite of this problem, it can be yours. I'll get the necessary papers ready."

"Father," the little nun cheerfully replied, "I don't worry about finding water. I'll leave that to Jesus. For now, let's settle with the paperwork so that I can have my children and my sisters here for the summer. The city is unbearable then. The fresh air will do everyone good."

That night, as Mother and her sisters prayed, they entrusted their new project to the Sacred Heart. "Dear Jesus, you have led us this far. Now you must lead us to the water we need. You are the Fountain of Life, and it is from you that all blessings flow."

The following day, the sisters went on a picnic in the woods. As they were walking along a path, Mother Cabrini tapped her walking stick on a patch of dirt and said in a very determined voice, "Have the men dig a well here. This is where our water will be found." The well was dug, and to this day, it has never gone dry! That summer, the children and the sisters enjoyed their new home in the country.

Manresa soon became known as The Sacred Heart Orphanage for Girls. Today it is known as St. Cabrini Home, West Park, and serves as a home for troubled teenagers. Teens are sent there from the court and live in a family-style setting with an adult in charge of each group home. The property also includes a cemetery for the sisters and an adult care facility.

17

ETERNITY TO REST

As Mother Cabrini stood on the hill watching the sun set over the Hudson River, her heart stirred within her. "Cecchina," she seemed to hear Father Dedé saying once more, "if you *really* want to be a missionary, then become one!"

Although Mother had been sent to work with the Italian immigrants in America, she never set limits to the generosity of her heart or her desire to share the love of Jesus. She reached out to anyone who needed her help. News of the Missionary Sisters and their work eventually echoed to far distant lands. Mother Cabrini began receiving letters and telegrams from bishops around the world asking her to send sisters to their dioceses. The needs were great, and Mother, urged on by the love of God, longed to meet them all. "Work my daughters," she urged her sisters, "for you have eternity to rest."

As the foundress of the Missionary Sisters of the Sacred Heart of Jesus, Mother Cabrini would often visit the missions where her sisters lived and labored. From the coal mines of Pennsylvania, to New Orleans' neighborhoods ravaged by yellow fever, from the silver mines of Colorado, to death row cells in New York State's Sing Sing Prison, Mother Cabrini and her sisters brought the love of God and his mercy. She crossed the ocean twenty-five times, establishing a total of sixty-seven missions spread over North and South America and Europe. During Mother's lifetime, she and her sisters overcame many difficulties in opening hospitals, orphanages, and schools throughout Italy and the United States and in England, France, Spain, Nicaragua, Brazil, and Argentina.

Mother Cabrini always believed very strongly in the dignity of women. She especially encouraged her sisters to offer women opportunities to learn skills that would help them support themselves and become productive members of society. In this she was far ahead of her time.

Throughout her life, Mother's fragile health continued to give her problems. It didn't help matters when she developed malaria while visiting the missions in Brazil. In 1917, Mother Cabrini, feeling very ill and tired, returned to Chicago. She hoped that doctors at Columbus Hospital, which she had founded, would be able to help her regain her strength. In spite of her own problems, she continued to worry about the health and safety of her sisters and the children in their care.

"Sisters, is everything ready for the children for Christmas?" the foundress anxiously inquired in late December.

"Not exactly, Mother," replied Sister. "We've just found out that Father Lombardi couldn't get the candy he wanted to give to the children."

"They must have candy for Christmas!" Mother insisted. "Visit Mr. Delicio and explain that I need some candy. Tell him that I'll be glad to pay for it. After all, Christmas is only a few days away. The children will be *so* disappointed if there's no candy. Ask Mr. Delicio if he can deliver it tomorrow. While I'm resting, I'll prepare the special treats."

On December 21, Mother Cabrini spent the day praying and preparing, with Sister Rita, the candy she had ordered for the children. "Mother, you need to rest," Sister Rita urged. "Everything is ready for the children. Now you must take care of yourself. The sisters can finish anything else you'd like done."

Shortly after noon on the following day, Mother Cabrini rang the little bell that she used to call for help. The sister who was caring for her found her sitting peacefully in her rocking chair. The soul that had loved Jesus so very much and had given her life to him, had quietly gone home to his heavenly kingdom. Mother Cabrini now had eternity to rest.

On July 7, 1946, just twenty-nine years after her death, Cecchina, the Lord's missionary, became the first American citizen (she had become a citizen in 1909) to be declared a saint.

18

THE DREAM CONTINUES

Since her death in 1917, the institute Mother Frances Xavier Cabrini founded has continued to answer the needs of the Church. Although Mother never personally went to China to minister to God's people, her sisters did. In 1926, six Missionary Sisters of the Sacred Heart of Jesus traveled to Shanghai to open schools. Twenty-three years later, the Chinese Communist government expelled all religious communities from the country. Many of the Chinese women who had answered God's call to become sisters were arrested and imprisoned for their Catholic faith. Others escaped in any way they could, often disguised as men.

The Missionary Sisters of the Sacred Heart have also carried Mother Cabrini's dream to Australia, Asia, and Africa, where they serve God's people in many different ways.

Since the very beginning of their institute, the Missionary Sisters have involved lay people in carrying out God's plan.

Today, in sixteen countries around the world, they continue, with many dedicated lay men and women assisting them, the wonderful work begun by Mother Cabrini.

Some of the institutions originally established by Mother Cabrini are no longer in existence. Others have changed to meet modern needs. The work of the Missionary Sisters is as varied as the individual and includes hospice, Elder Care programs, youth ministry, retreats, and advocacy and training for society's new immigrants. Those who are called to experience missionary life may also join the Cabrini Mission Corps as a volunteer. The sisters believe that wherever there is even one Missionary Sister of the Sacred Heart of Jesus, her work is blessed and made fruitful by the spirit of Saint Frances Xavier Cabrini. Each sister, living out her charism, helps and encourages everyone she serves to become one with her in the mission of Jesus.

PRAYER

Saint Frances Cabrini, when you were young, you dreamed of belonging to God in a special way. You had many obstacles to overcome, but you didn't let anyone or anything get in the way of your dream. Jesus and Mary became your best friends, and you counted on them to guide you in following your heart's desire.

I pray that I, too, may discover my dream and set my heart on its path, placing my trust in Jesus to help me see it through. Help me to remember that I can do all things in God who strengthens me.

Be my guide, Saint Frances, and pray to God for me.

Sacred Heart of Jesus, I place my trust in you. Amen.

GLOSSARY

1. **Benefactor**—someone who gives support to another. In most cases, the support is financial. Mother Cabrini's sisters relied on the generosity of others to help carry out their work.

2. **Bronchitis**—an inflammation of the airways of the lungs that makes it difficult to breathe and causes severe coughing.

3. **Buon giorno**—an Italian expression meaning "Good day."

4. **Capsize**—to turn upside down on the water.

5. **Charism**—the internal spirit of a person or a religious Order or institute. The charism is the inspiration of the Holy Spirit that sets the person or institute apart from others.

6. **Convent**—the name given to a house where religious sisters live.

7. **Delirium**—a temporary state of extreme mental disturbance that can be caused by fever or illness.

8. **Dormitory**—a large room (or an entire building) in which many people sleep.

9. Emigrate—the act of leaving one country to go and live in another. A person who does this is called an emigrant.

10. Friary—the residence of priests and brothers of certain religious Orders, such as the Franciscans and Dominicans.

11. Illiterate—unable to read or write.

12. Immigrate—the act of entering a new country in order to live there. A person who does this is called an immigrant.

13. La Madre—an Italian phrase meaning "Mother."

14. Lay person—any member of the Catholic Church who is not a priest, deacon, religious brother or sister.

15. Lire—a denomination of Italian money.

16. Mother Foundress—a woman who begins a religious Congregation or Order.

17. Rectory—a residence for priests.

18. Sacrifice—(as used in this book) something pleasing that we give up, or something difficult that we do to offer to God as a gift.

19. Signor—an Italian word meaning "Mr."

20. Signora—an Italian word meaning "Mrs."

21. Signorina—an Italian word meaning "Young Lady" or "Miss."

22. Smallpox—a very contagious disease caused by a virus. It produces a high fever and usually leaves scars on the skin.

23. Sodality—a Catholic organization whose members perform some charitable or spiritual works.

24. Stateroom—a large and well-furnished private cabin on a ship.

25. Strap—a leather belt used by farmers to chase away birds.

26. Vow—an important promise freely made to God. Members of religious Congregations make the vows of poverty, chastity, and obedience.

27. Your Eminence—a title of respect given to a cardinal of the Catholic Church.

28. Your Excellency—a title of respect given to a bishop.

29. Your Holiness—a title of respect given to the pope.

For more information about Saint Frances Xavier Cabrini and the Missionary Sisters of the Sacred Heart of Jesus, you may visit www.mothercabrini.com on the Internet.

Pauline
BOOKS & MEDIA

The Daughters of St. Paul operate book and media centers at the following addresses. Visit, call or write the one nearest you today, or find us on the World Wide Web, www.pauline.org

CALIFORNIA
3908 Sepulveda Blvd, Culver City, CA 90230   310-397-8676
2640 Broadway Street, Redwood City, CA 94063   650-369-4230
5945 Balboa Avenue, San Diego, CA 92111   858-565-9181

FLORIDA
145 S.W. 107th Avenue, Miami, FL 33174   305-559-6715

HAWAII
1143 Bishop Street, Honolulu, HI 96813   808-521-2731
Neighbor Islands call: 866-521-2731

ILLINOIS
172 North Michigan Avenue, Chicago, IL 60601   312-346-4228

LOUISIANA
4403 Veterans Memorial Blvd, Metairie, LA 70006   504-887-7631

MASSACHUSETTS
885 Providence Hwy, Dedham, MA 02026   781-326-5385

MISSOURI
9804 Watson Road, St. Louis, MO 63126   314-965-3512

NEW JERSEY
561 U.S. Route 1, Wick Plaza, Edison, NJ 08817   732-572-1200

NEW YORK
150 East 52nd Street, New York, NY 10022   212-754-1110

PENNSYLVANIA
9171-A Roosevelt Blvd, Philadelphia, PA 19114   215-676-9494

SOUTH CAROLINA
243 King Street, Charleston, SC 29401   843-577-0175

TENNESSEE
4811 Poplar Avenue, Memphis, TN 38117   901-761-2987

TEXAS
114 Main Plaza, San Antonio, TX 78205   210-224-8101

VIRGINIA
1025 King Street, Alexandria, VA 22314   703-549-3806

CANADA
3022 Dufferin Street, Toronto, ON M6B 3T5   416-781-9131

¡También somos su fuente para libros,
videos y música en español!